Dick Van Dyke

A Little Golden Book® Biography

By Christy Webster
Illustrated by Hollie Hibbert

A GOLDEN BOOK • NEW YORK

Text copyright © 2025 by Christy Webster
Cover art and interior illustrations copyright © 2025 by Hollie Hibbert
All rights reserved. Published in the United States by Golden Books, an imprint of
Random House Children's Books, a division of Penguin Random House LLC, 1745 Broadway,
New York, NY 10019. Golden Books, A Golden Book, A Little Golden Book, the G colophon,
and the distinctive gold spine are registered trademarks of Penguin Random House LLC.
rhcbooks.com
Educators and librarians, for a variety of teaching tools, visit us at RHTeachersLibrarians.com
Library of Congress Control Number: 2024940852
ISBN 978-0-593-80834-4 (trade) — ISBN 978-0-593-80835-1 (ebook)
Printed in the United States of America
10 9 8 7 6 5 4 3 2 1

Dick Van Dyke was born on December 13, 1925. He grew up in the city of Danville, Illinois. His mother, Hazel, was a stenographer, a person who writes down what people say in a courthouse. His father, Loren, was a baseball player, musician, and cookie salesman. When Dick was five years old, his brother, Jerry, was born.

Dick loved movies. On Saturdays, he would spend all day at the movie theater. His favorites were the comedies. He watched silent comedy stars like Buster Keaton and Laurel and Hardy. Then he would go home and try to imitate what he had seen.

In high school, Dick loved making people laugh by telling jokes and making funny faces. He also enjoyed singing, playing sports, doing magic, and performing in school plays.

Dick found the perfect after-school job for a budding entertainer—he worked as an announcer at the local radio station.

In 1944, he left high school during his senior year. The United States was involved in World War II, and young men Dick's age were needed to serve in the military. He decided to join the air force. At basic training, he took classes in many subjects and got good grades in all of them—except the ones he needed to be a pilot.

The air force assigned jobs based on what each person was good at. Instead of flying planes, Dick was placed in Special Services, the department that entertained the other troops. He helped put on shows and hosted a radio program.

After the war, Dick formed a comedy act called the Merry Mutes with his friend Phil Erickson. They told jokes and made up funny versions of popular songs, performing in clubs across the country. People liked their show, and Dick thought it was a great adventure, but money was very tight.

Dick and his girlfriend, Margie, wanted to get married, but they couldn't afford it. One day, in a California hotel, Dick met the producer of a radio show called *Bride and Groom*. In each episode, a couple would tell their love story and then have a wedding ceremony.

In 1948, Dick and Margie got married on the radio—while fifteen million people listened! The station paid for their wedding and honeymoon. Dick and Margie went on to have two sons and two daughters.

Soon after Dick and Margie's wedding, Dick and Phil got a regular spot doing their act in Atlanta, Georgia. While there, Dick started working on television, reading the news and also hosting a local variety show. He told jokes, made up skits, and interviewed people. Television had become very popular during and after the war. It was an exciting time to get into the business.

An old buddy from the air force helped Dick get an audition to be a TV host of *The Morning Show* on CBS. He got the job and in 1955 moved to New York City, where he worked alongside famous newsman Walter Cronkite.

Dick's television jobs changed often. He was taken off the news and became host of a cartoon show. Sometimes he was a guest star on comedies, and sometimes he hosted game shows. Nothing lasted very long.

Dick wanted to stay in show business, but since TV wasn't working out, he started auditioning for plays. When a casting agent asked if Dick could sing and dance, he said yes, even though it had been a long time since he had tried. Luckily, the audition went well! He was cast in his first Broadway musical, *The Girls Against the Boys.*

That show only ran for two weeks, but soon Dick was hired to play the role of Albert in a new musical called *Bye Bye Birdie*. He danced with Chita Rivera and sung "Put on a Happy Face." This show was a huge hit and won many awards—including one for Dick, who won a Tony Award for Best Actor!

Soon, someone who saw *Bye Bye Birdie* changed Dick's life forever.

Carl Reiner was a comedy writer that Dick admired. Carl wanted to make a television show about his own life. After watching *Bye Bye Birdie*, he decided Dick was perfect for the starring role. Dick read Carl's scripts and thought they were hilarious.

The new show premiered on October 3, 1961. They called it *The Dick Van Dyke Show,* even though most people hadn't heard of Dick . . . yet. The show followed his character Rob at home with his family and at the office with his funny coworkers.

It ran for five years and became one of the most beloved television series of all time!

Dick was a star, but he didn't go to many big Hollywood parties. He preferred being home with his children. He told an interviewer that if he acted in movies, he wanted them to be family movies. Walt Disney heard about this and cast Dick in his film *Mary Poppins.*

Dick played a chimney sweep named Bert. He sang "Chim Chim Cher-ee," did high-flying stunts, and danced with cartoon penguins. Dick thought it was amazing! So did moviegoers of all ages.

Dick made more and more movies, mostly comedies. He sang and danced again in *Chitty Chitty Bang Bang*, a musical about a flying car.

He was a bad guy in the 1990 movie *Dick Tracy*. The director knew audiences would be surprised with him playing the role of District Attorney Fletcher. No one would suspect a good guy like Dick Van Dyke!

In 2004, Dick returned to Danville High School to see the students perform *Bye Bye Birdie*. After the show, the principal presented Dick with his high school diploma, sixty years after he left school to join the air force. Dick was happy and proud.

Dick has continued to entertain people, even in his nineties. He appeared in *Mary Poppins Returns* when he was ninety-three years old. He performed in a gnome costume on the TV show *The Masked Singer* at age ninety-seven. And he dances every chance he gets!

Dick often calls himself lucky. He has said you need three things to enjoy a long life: "something to do, someone to love, and something to hope for. I had all those —and more!"

By sharing his amazing talent with the world, Dick Van Dyke never fails to make his fans feel lucky, too.